# THE POWER OF THE MIND CONSCIOUSNESS AND JOURNEY THROUGH THE INNER LANDSCAPE

How To Control And Master Your Mind?

How Much Can One Stretch It?

What Happens When The Mind Transcends its Limits And Gets Into A State Of Endless And Timelessness?

**ASEEM KR. KATOCH**

THE POWER OF THE MIND


ISBN


The Author holds the Copyright of this book. ©
Aseem Kr. Katoch

(Paper back version published on 11th July 2021)

DEDICATED TO THE MEMORY OF MY LATE
WIFE,
'UMA' WHOM I LOST AT HER PRIME

# ACKNOWLEDGMENTS

This book is a culmination of my desire, efforts, and inner calling. When I sat down to write this, it was only just myself and the solitude along with the universe and the 'Providence's blessings. Since the book is primarily about the power of the mind, consciousness, and journey through the inner landscape, it was but natural to get those moments of high vibrations and connect to the higher consciousness and other dimensions sometimes vibrating on different levels of energy. Me and my late wife 's years of expressions of gratitude to the universe and its creation and daily life out of which comes the abundance of feelings of wholeness as part of the larger cosmic whole. I knew that on this long and lone journey, like a wayfarer, I would need help, high energy, insights, and intuition that only God, the cosmic consciousness, and the Universe could help. From time to time in my moments of self-expression and gratitude, I earnestly prayed that man's consciousness to be goaded in the glory of God and for the greater good, universal love, compassion, and the welfare of mankind. As humanity is passing through a critical and uncertain time on one side and at another level due to the global pandemic, it needs a healing touch and the subtle power of the mind to be expanded for the greater glory and oneness of humanity.

I am thankful for the time, the Universe, the creation, the infinite source, which are part of the cosmos and seem to be the projection of the cosmic mind. **The surging waves of our mind are the reflections of our state in which we are vibrating.** I sincerely acknowledge the blessings, wishes of all who stood with me in these difficult times.  I am eternally grateful for the inspiration,    care, and concern, love, and compassion from my late wife Uma, an epitome of grace, intellect, and simplicity.

She was diagnosed with carcinoma with an advanced prognosis of the last stage. However, she went on to live five years contrary to high expert Doctors' opinions of only surviving for six months.  She overcame all this through the sheer power of her mind. Soon enough, the full-body scan showed her almost disease-free, which baffled the medical experts in the field. Sadly, I lost her on 5th February 2019. I was triggered to write this book sometime later in the year ending November 2020. It was those hard times when the entire world stood still due to prevailing pandemic, 'everything that is excellent or excruciating will come when this sleeping soul is aroused to self-conscious activity' at far East.

This just goes to show us that the power of the mind can be used through your subconscious mind to vanquish and overcome anything.
As Norman Cousin writes "I have learned never to underestimate the capacity of human mind and body to regenerate even when prospect seems most wretched."

 I am grateful to my precious child, who took the time to edit the many tiresome drafts of my book and put the manuscript in order. I thankfully acknowledge my mother and father's blessings with gratitude and love without which this milestone would not have been possible.  I would like to mention all other kind and generous people and thank them profusely for their love and support. I am grateful for those great minds whom I quoted and referred to in my book. Finally, my gratitude to the glory of God and its consciousness, which runs the show here on this Planet.


Author

"The greatest certainty of the Time is its uncertainty and for the Mind its eternity."


---- *Aseem Kr. Katoch*

## CONTENTS

<u>Chapter 1</u>

# THE  MIND - THE CONSCIOUSNESS

"Consciousness is the perception of what passes in man's own mind."

John Locke

Our understanding of the world is through our perception that reflects our consciousness, which is part of a completely larger Divine Consciousness. To know the mysteries of the World and the Cosmos through our cognitive faculties of knowledge, intellect, observation, contemplation, memory, reason, will, imagination, perception, and intuition will give us only a peripheral understanding unless we can perceive other dimensions transcending our five senses and light the flame of our consciousness with the Divine light. The deeper the awakening, the more the self-realization and understanding of the Universe and its creation through our subtle spiritual vibrations.

The mind—the consciousness is the ultimate gift to man, which has never been explored to its full potential. The mind, with its full concentration, intensity and focus can achieve anything as long as it is stretched till that stage. As William James writes "If you can change your mind, you can change your life"

The Universe is a panorama of endless movement and we are all connected with our inner self, and the cosmic world, through our consciousness called the 'mind'. The human mind is a complex phenomenon that can be changed, tamed, and programmed to meet the changing realities of time. You must stay connected with your inner self through your consciousness. That will keep you tranquil, and you will vibrate with high frequency, and your consciousness will look upon this world as an integral entity. Your Consciousness has that subtle power to attract all those forces, vibrating on the same frequency and same levels of vibrations, toward itself. You cannot experience any negativity at that stage and you tend to attract new possibilities, people, places, things, and circumstances. This all is an emanation from your consciousness as you are mastering your mind. You can also diminish the illusion of time and space and establish yourself in the glory of eternal and sacred truth.

In this world of mobility, that which comes, goes, humans are endowed with indomitable power of cognition or cognitive faculty that puts them on the highest pedestal than the rest of the creatures. Humans can unlock their power and potential through raising their consciousness by constant indulgence in the spiritual practice meditation of the infinite power. Either consciously or unconsciously, we have to choose a path that will gravitate towards a particular, idea, or goal. If we are constantly mindful of our mission and vision in life, concentrate on it, and take concrete action daily, we will be bound to succeed and the result would be no less anymore but in proportionate to our efforts. It is vital to vibrate on a higher frequency with positive energy. The human mind is scattered in all directions, with extreme divergent flows, negatives and it is not easy to tame the wavering thoughts of the mind, **as they are like surging waves in the ocean of motion.** We must vibrate on the highest level, and to reach that level, we must infuse our cognitive faculty with the supreme cognitive faculty also known as the infinite source or divine power, whatever you may call it. It is known that 'all the manifestations of the Universe are the varied expressions of the Divine energy'. In the Universe, the majority of the people generally live without any concrete goal, or any worthwhile thing to do except to get on with their daily rut leading mechanical lives. We are aware of our existence and our source of energy. A Zygote, in its nascent stage, is a weightless and extremely minuscule protein structure, which is a combination of mother's ovum and father's spermatozoa. This mass of energy soon turns into full-fledged life, which plays its role throughout, until it gets back to its source, and merges into the whole. This whole process is a creation, procreation from the unknown to known and has all its divine manifestation, and hence everyone is unique and has a different role to play in this vast body of creation. We all have come into this world for a purpose and how to find our purpose is our utmost purpose. To understand the Universal eternal truth and to able to vanquish your mind, Meditation or following a spiritual path is extremely important. Doing this will give you a feeling of equanimity, magnanimity, and calmness. Studies have suggested that doing simple meditation daily for even a few minutes can change the Gene expression of a human being.

There are many ambivalent thoughts, most of them are negatives, others confusing and conflicting—but whatever we continuously think, we become and create, we shape our world based on our daily thoughts, faiths, beliefs, and actions. As William James says "Most people live, whether physically, intellectually, or morally, in a very restricted circle of their potential being. They make very small use of possible consciousness".

Consciousness is a subtle form of energy or molecule of energy embodied in a body and subtle energy waves of infinite consciousness (non – local) beyond space and time. It is the stream of subtle cosmos energy, eternal and timeless capable of creating awe and wonder through the process of 'self- actualization' in the physical world followed by self-transcendence and self-realization. The evolution of the human through the constant process of the revolution of the consciousness is a pre-requisite for human growth and glory and societal social change. Consciousness, when limited to a spatial domain, is time-bound and is local because of the hardened conditioning of the whole body and the mind. This is where one gets into the narrow darkened state which doesn't allow the consciousness to evolve and navigate at a higher level, which gives rise to obscurantism. This is an anathema to realism. Reality is a state of consciousness depending upon individual experiences and hallucinations.

Since we as a human are part of the cosmological entity, we are all also part of the complete macrocosmic. Hence the Universe and the mind-the brain are in a process of constant expansion and change and so are the humans, in their process of consciousness-expanding or perfection-seeking merged with the cosmic consciousness. These are the questions which neither Scientists, Biologists nor Neuroscientists have been able to accurately answer. Only a spiritualist can realize them and solve this mystery. It is also important to mention that the inner landscape is suffused with such subtle energy and waves of molecules, the brain and the mind must correlate with its functioning but not causation. Hence, the endocrine glands have a profound impact on our emotions and the state of our consciousness. As you continue to think, think deeper, imagine, dream, desire, and use your intuition, cognitive faculties of perception, will power, memory, emotions to the maximum and prepare the mind for higher consciousness seek the answer for mundane existence and as you are in the majestic gate of the spiritual consciousness. So, at this conscious level, there is a thin line to cross this rubicon of your consciousness and merge with the spiritual consciousness. At this stage, you will continue to require the constant practice of meditation, to experience high frequency and vibration to rekindle your inner landscape and the crown chakra. You are at the cosmic gate and you will realize that all your dreams, desires, mission, vision, and goals, be of any sort, at that level can be easily accomplished just like by many of the great prophets, philosophers, inventors, sages, rishis, other men, scientists, writers, poets, painters, sculptors, composers, musicians that have had great insights, flashes because of transmutation of energy from the cosmic consciousness into the subconscious unit mind level consciousness.

# Chapter 2

# MIND:  THE UNEXPLORED TERRITORY

"In so far as the mind sees things in their eternal aspect, it participates in eternity"

Spinoza

In this world of time, space, persons, places, events, and circumstances, when we walk, talk and become indulgent, the process of conditioning starts within. The entire process starts hardening and gets cemented into our mind, thereby diluting the surging waves of the mind, and the mind will not be ready to accept any new thought unless you are willing to change the old attitude or pattern of your mind. We must be grateful that we have been given the chance to be born as humans and to realize our true potential, we must master our thoughts right from their conception, inception, to the stage of reception. There are truths and illusions in life, which we will encounter during this wonderful journey. The same also gets unfolded when we traverse ahead in this spatial sphere, which is relative. What is true for one may not be true for others unless he or she desires and believes it to be so. We must be mindful of the fact and the eternal truth that the 'Providence' has put you here for a 'purpose' and to make your entire journey of life sublime, you must know your intended purpose of where you are going and what are you doing.?

The Bible says 'knock and it shall be opened unto you," but the question that arises is, how many people truly knock?

One has to knock and not simply tap or touch the door, because no one will be able to hear it. Once you do it with clarity and with good positive intentions, a kind heart, an open mind, and gratitude, then you will receive what you have aspired for and the Universe will conspire to make it happen. No matter what, the Universe's response will certainly reach or react to your action. It is just as true as Newton's third law of motion. To every action, there is an equal and opposite reaction, and in turn, you will be able to serve truly those who seek. Life continues to give and return, which you must always think about and cherish. You must always treasure it.

Your goal or vision with a clear focus should be visualized, vitalized, emotionalized, and internalized. The entire visualization and internalization process is extremely important. Once things are internalized, and crystalized, it changes your internal dynamics, normative order, soon there is a 'paradigm shift', and then you can set a thought pattern in your desired direction.

During this entire process, you must continue to aspire for the intended goal or beyond. You must try to imagine, live, behave, act, react for all that you intend to be. As you continue to aspire for your goal or vision, it is like your ideation will continue murmuring about your goal. This paradigm shift would give you a clear and comprehensive description, redefine your life journey and your success is a foregone conclusion.

Mind is the most unexplored territory and has not been fully realized or used. The research goes on to show that humans have never used their mind to full potential and used up to a maximum of ten percent only in a few of the cases and in general, up to 4%. So far, humans have not been able to conquer their minds by any means whatsoever, save 'meditation' and other spiritual practices. The mind is bombarded with thousands of thoughts during the daytime, thoughts of varied kinds. There will be constant clash and cohesion at physical and psychic levels of these negatives, thoughts, and emotions unless it's not diluted and banished with positives; otherwise, it will continue to create chaos and confusion, which would lead to narrow, darkened, stagnated, and frustrating life ahead.

So beautifully, Albert Einstein writes 'Strange is our situation here on Earth. Each of us comes for a short visit, not knowing why yet sometimes seeming to divine purpose.'

The mind has to be in perfect control. Of all the living creatures on the planet, the human mind is the most complex and complicated. It is like an ocean of waves. You must fill in it with the most positive inspiring thoughts, positive words, and march on to accomplish great things which you intend to do or fit in the greater scheme of your grand plan or things that are part of this Universe.

The Humans on this Planet are bestowed with intellect, intelligence, and intuition and they must make use of them instead of sitting idle and relying only on fate, you must be vigorously active, action-oriented mode, indulgent, and positive. That is the magic of happiness and mantra of success. You have to awaken the cognitive faculty latent in your mind. And you might ask, how should one do that? It can be by the right approach, right-thinking, use of intention, expectation, perception, intuition, willpower, and imagination. What differentiates the human from the beast? Animals also do possess motor or sensory organs, like humans, but humans are endowed with cognitive faculties and the power of thinking, which if used effectively and realistically, can create magic and wonders at all levels of human existence.

# Chapter 3

## MASTER YOUR MIND

"The mind is everything, what you think you become."

Buddha

According to ancient wisdom, the existence of human beings is not a single or random event in the evolutionary dynamics or spheres. The mind is the most powerful weapon yet, it is also the most ignored and neglected, and if it is not mastered and trained, the human psyche gets shrunken, as the mind is not a tangible thing like the brain.

Mind is the master of perceiving things and such acts. But, it is done with the help of the other sensory and motor organs. Perception, these sensory organs act as a vehicle and help the mind in assimilating the five factors i.e ethereal factors, aerial factors, luminous factors, liquid factors, and solid factors.

The mind is subtle and it controls the brain. It's the subject and the brain is the object and it cannot be destroyed. It is the transformed state of consciousness. For the action, the mind transcends and acts through the sensory and motor organs. Your mind is the ultimate cause of knowing. Any analysis or introspection within the domain of mind and any action you propose to do will only be bigger through your constant thought, which you have created in your mind. As the mind turns out to be doers of the thought, it is important to work on positive affirmations. Once you master your mind and master your energies, only then you will be able to strive for excellence in any area of your existence. As Napolean Hill writes "Whatever the mind of man can conceive and believe, it can achieve."

The mind perceives what is being observed, practiced, and constantly being thought. The entire Universe is oceans of waves and energy of varied levels such as the physical level, psychic level, and spiritual level. Whatever you perceive are the waves of varied energy of the universe. The thought process, your perception, and your action will trigger your move. Whatever, you think and feel, the mind will process the same. To take yourself to a higher plane, it is essential for you to come out of your conditioned mind and into the present moment and the state of silence and emptiness. You must connect to your inner self to move into another dimension. It is important to reprogram and elevate your mind by meditation and divine practices.

The mental rehearsals strengthen mental related pattern, cognitive thinking, and other internal states. Mental rehearsals also installs the circuit in the Brain that the events have already occurred. The human body is a colony of one hundred trillion cells, besides brain circuits of one hundred billion neurons, a gigantic network of 'electromagnetic currents'.

The entire process begins with dynamic and creative force while you are on a continuous journey the lone word faith and beliefs as you hold to these words into your mind and move ahead with clarity, purpose, and mission in life.

"If you do everything as if it were the last thing you were doing in your life and stop being aimless, stop  letting your emotions override what your mind tells you. Stop being hypercritical, self-centered, irritable. If you can manage this, that is all even the Gods can ask of you," says Marcus Aurelius, the Roman Emperor.

As long as our mind is a mystery, the universe, the extended consciousness of our mind reflects the cosmic mind will also be a mystery.

# Chapter 4

# LEVELS OF THE MIND

"When the mind is thinking, it is thinking to itself."

Plato

The Conscious Mind, which operates within five sensory organs: eyes, ears, nose, tongue, and skin having desire or aversion to stimuli.

It is the conscious mind, which is the thinking mind and can feel the difference between good and bad, positive and negative, and can take decisions based on thinking and consciousness. Ancient wisdom tells us that the ten sensory and motor organs are like wild horses, if harnessed, they will bring energy to the mind. Our pain and pleasure, our actions and reaction are based on the desire of our conscious mind. Human beings mostly act based on their conscious minds.

The subconscious mind is the storehouse of what has been penetrated to it through the conscious mind. It is the storehouse of your emotions, thoughts, reflections, and memories. The subconscious mind is the most expanded than the conscious mind. It is the more creative mind and can think and vibrate on a higher philosophical level. The subconscious mind serves all of your dreams. All further hypnotic inferences are the creation of the subconscious mind. According to Freud, the imagery of dreams can be interpreted through psychoanalysis, to understand the true nature and dynamics of the mind. As stated before, the Universe is nothing but oceans of energy, vibrations, and waves. We perceive nothing but the energy of varied length.

The subconscious mind has the power to influence the conscious mind, which entertains and governs the thought process of any human being, once it has developed very strong and emphatic, impeccable beliefs. The subconscious mind cannot tell the difference between positive and negative, real and imagined thoughts or any image or picture. What you consistently and continually think of will eventually manifest in your lives.

"Whatever we plant in our subconscious mind and nourish with repetition and emotions will one day become reality," writes Earl Nightingale.

The superconscious mind goes beyond all the conscious levels of the mind. There are extremely few who can get into this subtle psychic realm. This is the realm of high intuition and creative insight beyond the creativity of the subconscious mind. It has been found and studies suggest, that many of the creative acts—a flash of genius, insight has engaged from this layer of the mind.

Many poets, artists have discovered something by way of intuition.

The elevation of mind can be experienced through meditation and higher practice of spirituality and divinity, which can also be traced to deep extrasensory perception in the rarest of the rare case. If one has to attain this exalted state, they have to feel the vibration, waves of the universal, and to perceive all creations and get into the realm of the infinite and perceive energy from ashes to stars and cross the fabric of space and time. The universe is nothing but a vibrational play of energy, frequency, and vibrations.

Sit with like-mind people, if you are not with the teacher or mentor, then get with the teachings. Read books to lift your mood and mind. To read is to voyage through time. As Plato writes "Books give a soul to the Universe, wings to the mind, flight to the imagination and life to everything."

Besides this, the human brain consists of some other critical structures in the form of the brain Beta Waves. The brain produces beta waves thus waking our consciousness conditions such as our intuition, telepathy, creativity, etc.

Alpha waves are also emanated from the brain. Ancient wisdom, scientists, and sages have said that the energy of alpha waves increases calmness and tranquillity. The same is viable for the development and Control of Chakras, glands in that state of equanimity.

In Meditation, action, and efforts as brain waves are vibrating on the high frequency with corresponding to what has been visualized and internalized and this process is flawless. One must be mindful that from the base of the spine and running upwards to the crown of the head there are more than seven energy centers called chakras, which oversee and control the mind and body. These energy centers can be perceived and felt, during meditation and through constant practice, one can elevate or stretch his mind as much as one can.

To get beyond the bounds of matter, space, and time and to diminish this illusion, one must concentrate his physical, psychic, and spiritual energies toward an infinite source. That exalted state of mind can only be attained and realized through your inner journey of consciousness into the inner landscape, as it starts, from hypnosis, hallucination to intuitive thoughts and much more creative, intuitive thought, thereby increasing our consciousness and stretching into timeless and infinite space.

Chapter 5

# CONSCIOUSNESS AND JOURNEY THROUGH THE INNER LANDSCAPE

"Become who you are."

Friedrich Nietzsche

Humans are the most advanced, evolved species on this planet than other creatures and are bestowed with the infinite power of intelligence and thinking. They simply need to think in the right perspective and shift their mental paradigm and propel mental propensities toward their goal and envision the future of their choice and concentrate on the present moment. They must do what they love to do and whatever they are passionate about and dedicate their lives to it. All future events and possibilities will keep unfolding and they can accomplish all desire things in their lives.

The human mind is the ultimate gift to man. How can we feel the existence of the mind? The mind can feel external objectivities and respond to external stimuli. As everything in the Universe is energy, the energy in its subtle form is consciousness, and this consciousness feels the mind. This consciousness can be broadened by constant practice and indulgences in positive fruitful pursuits and larger societal interests. The mind is mostly prone to negative thinking due to its strong conditioning, and other environmental factors, associations, habit, circumstances. As you continue to think, you are constantly speaking to your mind, and in the process, you are processing and programming it with your thoughts. This thinking is being cemented to your consciousness and in the inner landscape in all its form, action, and vibration. It becomes a vital force to be reckoned with.

From conception to perception, all is within you. We get connected with everything through our minds. We create a mental picture and imagination of our desire things and then sow the seeds of success, failures, fears within. Essentially it is the mind in our inner landscape that is the greatest repository of infinite power, and to utilize it to its full power, potential, and experience, its extensity with intensity and shine to the fullness of its true glory through imagination, intuition, and will power, incantation, ideation of your goal, and by the process of auto-suggestion. The process of auto-suggestion is a kind of self-communication internally to speak within your mind. It is wise to do this process intensely and with deep incantation, as it will program your subconscious mind. It is indispensable for taking you toward your desired goal and vision. The principle of auto-suggestion is of prime significance in the entire process of your journey as it would set, the paradigm shift, and the mind would be consummated with your dominant thought and it would vibrate with high frequency. This thought becomes an inextricable part of your sub-consciousness mind.

It is at this stage that the inner landscape is fully ripened and the seeds which you have sown and internalized will now fully germinate to their physical equivalent. Then the most tenuous state comes easily within the grasp of the individual. These prime dominant thoughts are emotionalized, the blissful wave will engulf the mind, this will further permeate into the subconscious mind. In the vast ocean of mind, all waves of imagination, creation would be there.

The HUMAN mind is extraordinarily powerful. Some are more extraordinary and constantly preoccupied with thoughts of all sorts. When the human mind is free from the maddening rush of negative thoughts, clashes, disturbances, or anxiety and there is fulsome equanimity, it vibrates on a high frequency and can be connected to other dimensions. The intuitive faculty is the natural consequence of your being in a higher state of consciousness. It is like a flash of light will come from the soul or spirit, when your mind is calm, and position to sense or receive and send thoughts there is nothing much to experience except intuition, depending upon the degree of thoughts vibrations. There are 'hunches' one is known to the experience of the coming events or fortune. To understand the essence of infinite or divine consciousness, it is vital to explore and stretch the mind and journey through the inner landscape. As R.W. Emerson said, "That only which we have within, can we see without."

# Chapter 6

## THOUGHTS, FEELINGS, DREAMS, AND TIMELESSNESS

"The most necessary task of civilization is to teach how to think?"

Thomas A Edison

Incubate an idea and set your dream high. Your dreams must soar. Whatever you wish to do and want to accomplish in life must be consciously planted beforehand in your mind. Write it down clearly and precisely, knowing that to have all these things, there is a price that you will have to pay.

Before you go to school, read and consciously think about your goal. The majority even do not think what they think. As George Bernard Shaw writes "Two percent of the people think, three percent of the people think, they think and ninety-five percent of the people would rather die than THINK.

As you are constantly thinking and visualizing it, try to create an image of your dream, whether you want to be a writer, scientist, leader, motivator, dreaming to change the societal dynamics by enunciating new intellectual ideological revolution, a dream house in space, dream castle, dream vacation beyond space and time dimension or wanting to set any benchmark, you can. Dream mind is exploratory and insightful about the events, situations, and equations more than the simple awaking mind. A mind constantly thinking about the goal or vision, how lofty it is if it nourishes with the repetitive thought process, feelings and emotions are sure to become one day a reality.

James Allen writes "The dreamers are the saviors of the world. Humanity cannot forget its dreamers; it cannot let their ideals fade and die. The world is beautiful because they have lived; without then humanity would perish."

Deirdre Barrett, a psychology professor, says that "people turn to their subconscious minds to get answers to their problems and ponder over the question just before falling asleep".

**Make your dreams part of your thought process, cherish your dreams and visions, nourish them and immerse in them, the success will come unexpected hours unconsciously.**

Human existence is precious. We cannot afford to lose any moment of time or any fraction on baseless follies. As discussed in previous chapters once, you have control over your mind and have been able to program your subconscious mind, which is the storehouse of emotions. all seem within your limits.  What we think is important. Any idea or thought that crosses our mind or that we consciously entertain and want to give a definite shape. How should we use our minds for fulfilling our desires and create deliberate coincidences, co-creations? Thoughts keep recurring, traveling, and run continuously as long as our mind is active. This is how the mental paradigm functions once you program it through daily practice and habits. Now you are completely in a different state of equilibrium. You must rest your past, leave it behind completely, and be in a 'now' moment, and be tuned to the new future possibilities. There is no competition but creation, and self-expansion, no jealousy, save joy, and harbor no grudge. Look for the possibilities of building new bridges, thorough creation and not a competition and generate wealth. Entertained the thoughts, work on them with complete focus, and do not get distracted by any other idea. Thought is creative energy and you should immediately put yourself into action. Stick to your purpose and pursuits with gratitude as you realize that there is no other time than now. Do not ever overthink how to do it and of the future. Just act on it and do not bother about what has happened, as yesterday is history. Instead, straighten your present vision and hold on to it. Hold on to this thought steadfastly and consciously act on it with strong belief with unwavering faith.

Our mind is constantly occupied with thoughts and cannot remain idle. It will keep forming varied images of different objects, places, persons, things, and events throughout as long as it's active. Thousands of other thoughts will keep flashing in our minds ranging from cursory to dominant thoughts. These thoughts are nothing but waves of subtle energy as there is a constant flow of this energy and bundles of positive or negative energy that has been formed and processed. If you have mastered your mind, you will be in a position to keep your mind floating or drooling in positive thoughts. It is vital for you at this stage to keep your mind engaged in positive pursuits of life, broaden your consciousness, and connect it to the other dimension of the infinite source. It is not easy to have positive thoughts all the time, the contrary is true. One can easily be swayed away by any negative opinions, gossips, newspaper, television, and media reports. Just like how healthy food is good for the body, healthy and positive thoughts are essential for the wellbeing of the mind. As there is a constant cycling of these thoughts in your mind, that will give shape to the imagery and will pass on the same to the subconscious mind. Once they are part of the subconscious mind, they will become your primary and dominant thought energy and will pass the same energy to the Universe's divine source from where you are originated.

This transmutation of positive thought energy to the universal energy can be done by a constant process of auto-suggestion and method of ideation and incantation. Then the subconscious mind will produce results, exactly the way you want. If one can master the process in its entirety and reprogram its inner landscape, the desired result is a foregone conclusion. This will certainly put you on the highest pedestal and you will be well on your way to realize your dream, goal, and vision.

As you know the human body's entire dynamics are based on a totality of factors, and once you take control of your mind and thoughts, you are halfway through. The rest half requires single-minded pursuits coupled with your imagination and willpower, perception, intuition and if you are relentless and steadfast, you will surely be victorious. That is the power of the mind and thought. You will have an abundance of energy if you're willing to travel the extra mile. Those who can master this art have the greatest happiness, wealth, and art of innovation. In this Universe, everything is controlled by cause and effect. The law of cause and effect is so strong that the effect of a particular cause becomes the potent cause of the next stage. The more deeply we think and go inwards, we get the subtler mind. By constant practice of thinking about your larger goal of life, whether you want to become a global business icon, inventor, writer, painter, musician, explorer, global leader, motivator, you can explore the possibilities of infinite sources by your sixth sense. Just as the effect of a cause becomes the cause of the next stage, so is the effect of your thought. What is the cause of your reason to and boundless source of energy to be permeated in the sub-consciousness mind, which would be fully ripened and believed to be true, success, is a foregone conclusion?

Thought is subtle energy, a kind of an 'ectoplasm'. This term was coined by Psychical researcher Charles Richet (Professor Charles Robert Richet) in 1894. He was a French physiologist and a noble prize winner in physiology. When thought is entertained projected internally, it takes the form of feelings, in a very subtle level of energy. Thought is feeling and that is nothing but energy, a subtle level of energy, so all of us are in the same level of energy and vibrate on the same form. In this system of thought processes, it is essential to connect with your infinite source or sixth sense to get an answer for your fundamental existential question and seek a way to navigate across it. So, pursue positive dominant thoughts with a firm incantation to permeate the same dominant thought with a full conviction and belief into the subconscious mind. The miracles will start unfolding as your subconscious mind is your most powerful weapon to process and act upon the same.

Thought is such a pivotal source of energy that releases the energy wave and gets merged with other energy waves of the cosmos. It is like cosmic energy or cosmic wave in the vast ocean of your mind.

**James Allen so beautifully writes "Your vision is the promise what you shall one day be; your ideal is the prophecy of what you shall at last unveil"**

The way you think will make you a winner or loser. As your actions are being propelled by your thought, they are a guiding force behind your action and positive and sentient thoughts must be entertained. Since man is neither beast nor god and is easily swayed away by people's opinions, judgments,  consciousness must be broadened and linked with other dimensions of life. When something drastically goes wrong if you are a constant victim of a negative thought, emotional upset and not able to control your mind and seem to be drooling yourself in a complete darkened state, you will try to look and see solace in other comparable occasions or situation of like-minded men found much in the majority. Sometimes each of us momentarily entangled in a perturbation common to all.


You must aspire for higher and beyond your goal, yearn for unlimited things, moving from known to unknown mangling your thought energy with the source energy of this Cosmos. This will change your mental paradigm, as you are emotionally involved with your dream, vision, and goal. This emotional surge in the subconscious mind will propel your propensities and conspire to work for the completion of your mission or any undertaking you have undertaken in your life. Your single dominant thought will become the source of your creativity and will throw you to the shore of other times in your dreamland. There will be timelessness in the pursuit of this eternal journey. You are in the moment of ecstasy as you have not created only such a great, vital subtle force by the virtue of your eternal blissfulness but also connected yourself to the higher dimension and your source.

You may do whatever you wish to desire or generate a wealth of any amount by this practice and by applying the principle of autosuggestion, perception, intuition, willpower, and imagination. You may if you wish and desire to explore and goad into the unknown kingdom of Infinite source through the power of sub-consciousness and superconscious mind, where you would be beyond the fabric of space and time. Where you can perceive anything between stones and stars that is at a supra-mundane level. This is the power of mind if channelized fully is like laser and can permeate and penetrate Cosmos and into other dimensions. This is fulsome human existence and wholesome existential liberation.

Chapter 7

## PARADIGM SHIFT AND CONTROL YOUR MENTAL FACULTIES

"If you want small changes in your life, work on your attitude. But If you want big and primary changes, work on your paradigm."

Stephen Covey

The human mind does not remain tamed or subdued long and seeks freedom. Its faculties such as perception, intuition, reasoning, imagination, and will if not used or put into operation would become dormant and the entire mental desideratum would not vibrate on high frequency and same will be engaged in petty thoughts and things around. We must not allow it to slip into the whirlpool of negativity, prejudice, hatred, ill will, or any sort of contempt, ridicule. Whatever you see, you perceive, you conceive and recreate that thing in your mind.

In this Universe everything moves, the nature of the universe is dynamic. The origin and possible end of the creation have to meet from where they have originated. So, the world is dichotomous having two sides of things, like good, bad, beautiful, ugly, male and female white, black. These dichotomies are further dissected if you wish it so. But essentially it remains at two levels. Accordingly, thought is also of similar dichotomous nature, good thought, bad thought, positive and negative thoughts. Those who constantly and consistently master this practice of positive thoughts have reached the pinnacle of success. It is also important during this entire process as you chant or incant your gigantic goal mantra, sometimes your inner mind operates in the periphery of time-space and person, and by your actional faculties (action towards your goal ) you can get what you want. So here you are possessed with the indomitable power of imagination, perception, intuition, will, and a strong desire to reach your goal. You need to tune into and focus toward the set goal with a single pursuit of determination and willpower to invoke your mental cum actional faculties. This would set you apart from the rest and you will find yourself in the category of the exalted group of individuals, who have that consuming burning desire to reach and meet their goals. In a dichotomous world, your action is connected with a temporal, spatial, and personal level. Your show up on this Earth is not accidental but with a definite purpose and without any limitation, and limitation if any is of your mind due to social cum environmental and conditioning of the mind and other factors including education, which gives more information less of learning and skill not equipped to shape your mind. The law of the Universe and ancient wisdom says that humans can achieve anything at a temporal,  spatial level by dint of one 's consistent pursuit and yearning for the goal. These faculties will keep you attached to your goal and propel you to move forward and give you all desired things such as health, wealth, fame, glory, success, power, and position in life.  In doing so, if you enjoy and got it what you desire and also wish to give and share your wealth, knowledge, and all that you enjoy in this voyage until your destination, and are grateful for the infinite power. You have been given chance to use your full capacities in whatever capacity you can.

If you want to break this dichotomous knot and wish to travel beyond the fabric of time and space and get connected with source power, the spirit you have to offer your mind to the source leaving your vanity and other actional faculties behind to be more devotional, grateful, and surrender mode. You would feel ecstatic beyond the joy of the material world into the spiritual world.

The human body, the more subtle and at the same time very complex thing is the "mind". Our knowledge and contact with many of these things around us or in this universe are not at the physical level but through our mind, through our nerve cells, nerve fibers. When you think of anything, we feel things in our mental image which is an internal projection with the help of our nerves. This seems all mysterious but unraveled mysteries of the mind and its terrific power which seems to have answers for everything within the human mind. The science of applied psychology can give you the best idea about this if one is keen to explore it further and this could further be realized as you connect with yourself and with the divine power.

# Chapter 8

# AUTO-SUGGESTION INCANTATION AND OUTER SUGGESTION

"Speak your latent conviction, it shall be universal sense, for the inmost in due time becomes the outmost."

R.W. Emerson

Autosuggestion done through your incantation is an extraordinary and powerful process. If it becomes a habit more so of external habits and it becomes natural. When auto-suggestion becomes your nature and can be repeated in your unconscious mind, use your incantation as your desired goal. This continuous repetition daily, particularly at night, during sleeping time, will influence the subconscious mind. If you are doing it with a great deal of passion, emotions, these auto suggestions are inextricably linked to your goal and have taken the shape of nature as the persistent ideation of your goal through incantation. Autosuggestion is done by the self or it is instilled during the process, outer suggestion does hold importance also. The outer suggestion comes from a good company like the community you are living in, the time being spent with the people around you create different thought process and you should make sure that you do not spend time with a bad company. A good company's energy and vitality will be a greater influence on your thinking and everything and it will stretch your autosuggestion. So outer suggestion is equally important and indispensable. For your autosuggestion and realization of your desired goal, you must select your friend, company, and mastermind group keeping your goal, vision in your mind. This process is vital, as it would re-program the inner landscape of your subconscious mind in such a way that would facilitate your success easily. The autosuggestion will strengthen your subconscious beliefs. Since you are so attached and have become emotional with your desired goal and constant and consistent process of autosuggestion through deep incantation, ideation. Your subconscious mind is entirely engulfed with emotions and your subconscious beliefs have become so strong that nothing can stop you from reaching your desired goal. Once you have mastered the art of developing your beliefs first by honoring commitment through constant practice of disciplining your mind and positive thought process leaving no scope for any negatives to enter your mind. Further, the 'Reticular Activating system' (RAS) of the Brain clears the information and plays a central role in states of consciousness like alertness and sleep.  Antonio Damasio, Neuroscientist and prof of psychology, philosophy, and Neurology  has shown that 'emotions play a central role in states of consciousness or social cognition  and decision making.'  The other process such as thought, habit, and autosuggestion with incantation as train your subconscious mind impeccably and stretch you toward your goal turning you unconsciously genius and workaholic.

Patanjali, the great Indian Sage, and Philosopher had mentioned about 2000 years ago in one of his aphorisms ( sutras)  that the human mind has got more than  50 main propensities and is working in different directions both inside and outside almost ten different directions. They work within and without, internally and externally and these propensities are controlled by the pineal gland. This pineal gland is also called 'the third eye' Crown Chakra  (Sahashar in Sanskrit ) for many reasons as it is located in the center of the brain. That allows the pervasive power if it awakens or arisen by doing meditation and serves as a metaphysical connection between the physical and spiritual world as ancient wisdom and spiritual traditions say so. Since we all are operating within the periphery of time and space so are the other objects save the spirit and infinite source. This moment has been here for millions of years and more. Just as the ' Sun " is the nucleus, the center of the ' Solar System', so is the human mind. It has an unfathomable capacity to create anything first in the psychic realm, then in the form of imagination and dream, and then actualize the same into the physical realm. (physical form). This actual progress toward your goal through the process of ideation, incantation, and strong subconscious beliefs and by your persistent action. The subconscious beliefs and constant and consistent autosuggestion have become nucleus centers to propel you toward your goal. Simultaneously your mind would continue to soar high and high and vibrate at higher frequency as you continue to overcome all your limitations, tossing and vacillating between finite and infinite spheres. As Richard Bach writes "If we follow our dream we can truly soar." It is at this stage you feel your mental faculties such as intuition, imagination soar and are beyond time and space continue to imagine the unimagined.

The man sees all the easiest, who dream highest. As you develop your imagination and also the art of visualization, as you engage yourself intellectually with an intuitional faculty and conscious and unconscious portion of your mind, nothing would stand in the way of your goal.

# Chapter 9

# GOAL, HAPPINESS, AND BLISSFULNESS

"If you want to live a happy life, tie it to a goal, not to people or thought."

Albert Einstein

What are the guiding philosophy and guiding principles that propel you toward your goal? You must know where you are and where you are going. Once the goal is set, then you must inculcate a code of discipline. Adhering to the discipline means seventy percent of success. It is a strict regimen strictly to be followed, coupled with firm determination to reach your goal. In this process, the body, the mind, and control over sensory and motor nerves are important. The mind gets compartalized, when you see, hear, smell as one position takes the objective form and the other takes the subjective form. In the recreation of something memorable, there must be a repetition of your goal so that you cannot lose sight of it. Stillness and suspension of mind are equally important as a creative state comes from stillness like the sprout beneath the ground comes out its own in harmony with nature. That the eternal wisdom that flows through you what is seen and manifested in its physical form and what is sensed and experienced dilute the worlds of duality and its dichotomous nature. The glory of your mind stretches on and on and all desired things seem to be within your limits.

As Aristotle writes " Happiness is the settling of the soul into its most appropriate spot."

Blissfulness and happiness are vital for harmonious relationships with all other dimensions of life and it also makes your journey even within and to overcome the difficulties and challenges on the voyage. If you are feeling sad, grumpy, off, despondent that would mean nothing worthwhile can be done in that mental state. You must practice positive affirmation with new thoughts, ideas, and insights, which would be a facilitator in this process. Practice and emotionalize the entire process of your being. Never lose sight of your goal, keep reminding yourself of your intended target. Happiness is the state of mind, the subjective activity that enjoys happiness is the mind. Happiness is such an important aspect that the entire body cell's mood is in perfect harmony inclusive of nerve cells and nerve fibers. It is the mind that seeks most happiness in all levels, physical, mental, intellectual, intuitional. Since everything in the

Universe is energy and vibrational. The existence of anything in the world is based on frequency and vibration. These vibrational experiences are felt, enjoyed by your mind. So the vibrational sphere must be balanced by positive thoughts and subconscious beliefs and negate the negatives and other disbeliefs, which you had already built over the years by your habit and conditioning. You can re-program your subconscious mind through the process of auto-suggestion. The seeds of happiness are sown the day you embark on your goal relentlessly and with a single-minded dedication. This entire process on the way toward your dream would bring a major mental paradigm shift and give you so much elation as it is opening new vistas in your life by unfolding the unknown and creating strong possibilities of a bright future. Further, your faith and beliefs do control your action and behavior. As Bruce H. P Lipton writes "Beliefs control your behavior and gene activity and consequently unfolding your lives." Happiness has largely to do with your enthusiasm and preoccupation with other pursuits. Besides your vision and mission in life. It generally with the person who is busy, and also has a larger societal interest in mind rather than his own. Happiness gives you the fulsome feelings of life and its existence. You continue to vibrate a high frequency of positive vibrations and willing to go an extra mile in pursuit of your goal and other larger interests. Happiness is largely connected to your impersonal pursuits such as doing something for a cause rather than your aggrandizement. The real pursuit of happiness is when you are making others happier by touching their lives through kindness, love, care, compassion, and sharing. The enormity of the same you would feel in your life and you will always be in your best of times and happiness.

Chapter 10

# MIND THE CREATOR AND THE MAKER

"Vision with Action can change the world."

Nelson Mandela

Your mind must constantly ideate on your goal and the goal must be aligned with your vision. Since the mind tends to travel and be occupied with past events, good or bad or whatever it might be, it easily sabotages your mission and goal you are inclined to pursue. You must sacrifice a great deal and willing to lose comforts for your vision. You must get rid of all boredom and distress and march ahead with a single focus on your goal and vision. You must have clarity of two things, first, you must be clear on your purpose and mission and its target meaning where you are and where you would be going? How to put mind, body, and brain into action mode. The relationship is symbiotic. When you realize and actualize the true meaning of your existence through the self-awareness and self-actualization process, and feel other dimensions, you start to realize and liberate

53

your great potential. In other words, "Self-actualization is possible only as side effects of self-transcendence." writes Vikotre E.Frankl in his book Man's search for meaning.

Mind is dynamic and cannot remain stagnant and this movement is from crude to subtle and in the process of self-actualization and self-transcendence, it is on its way to greater self-discovery. Your consciousness, which is a part of the cosmic cognitive faculty expands in all directions in the vastness of this creation, you become a goldmine of knowledge and wisdom and the Universal love personified. This is aligned with the principles of  Abraham Maslow's proposed characteristics of "self-actualization and other basic needs of safety, belonging. Self-esteem first needs to be satisfied before being fully able to realize one's genius, creativity, and humanitarian potential along with intellectual purpose,  great responsibility with a duty to accomplish a particular mission in life, creative spirit, good moral intuition, peak experiences, humanitarianism, efficient perception of reality, purpose, equanimity, authenticity, and acceptance". Self-actualization and self-transcendence along with self-realization man are capable of defying and delaying even the worst possible conditions perceivable. Once you define your vision and dream and proceed with the expansiveness of the human mind move from being selfish to selfless. As Viktor E. Frankel elegantly writes "And what about man? Are you

sure that  the  human world is a terminal point in
the evolution of the Cosmos?"  As all thoughts,
ideas, objects arise out of the human mind and to
obviate all possibilities of physical and psychic
clash with any other entity or object, the cure is
self-transcendence  through  the  process  of
stillness, meditation, and self-realization and seek
refuge and merge with the cosmic mind. That is
the state of liberation and cosmic bliss beyond the
domain of mundane pleasures and pains and
other existential desires. This answers a question
as  Frankel posed in his book 'Man's searching for
meaning'  "it is not conceivable that there is still
another dimension, a world beyond man's world,
a word in which  the question of an ultimate
meaning of human suffering would find an
answer."

# Chapter 11

## STRETCH YOUR MIND

"If we want to change our lives, we need to stretch our minds."

Dr.    Wayne Dyer

The mind is not where you are, what you think and do. You have to engage it and preoccupy it with good thoughts, feelings, and emotions. The creative faculties within you are unique and we simply need to learn to use them. You must stretch your mind as much as you can and the more you stretch it, the more it fetches the desired things. The mind is never used to its full potential and it is estimated that five percent of the population uses its minuscule level up to five to ten percent only. Why is it not used? The reason is being that the majority have no clarity where they are and where they want to go, no clear-cut goal, objective, vision in life, and worthwhile things to work on. You have been conditioned to think right from an early age followed by education, which is more information-based than knowledge, no training or stretching of mind, which makes you act mechanically,  play, and stay within your comfort zone.  You become slack and snoozy in your mental paradigm and the process, you form a poor self-image of yourself in tune with your daily rut and routine of life. As T.S Eliot writes "Where is the knowledge we have lost in information". "Only those who will risk going too far can possibly find out how far one can go".

The question is how to use our mind in a controlled way and at the same time creatively and productively first by lifting ourselves in all spheres of life be it physically, mentally, economically, and spiritually?  It is important to construct the new and deconstruct the old poor picture of the mental image of yourself. You have to engineer it with the new mental paradigm, energy, frequency, and vibrations.  As you know your mission and target that has to be achieved and all the reasons you need to work vigorously and fiercely until you achieve your desired goal. Keep the act, action, simple straight, judge less, listen more,  and ponder, pause, introspect and enjoy the mystery.  The insight you gain and the creative pursuits are part of a larger whole that flows through you.  Since your finiteness is inextricably linked with the infinite and in the process,  you must think about the result and the rest that will be taken care of by the universal energy or the infinite source.

It is interesting to point out here that when you are in that exalted state of being, when you have moved on from being selfish to selfless and treasure more in giving in terms of love, kindness, knowledge, and other pursuits which have a large societal impact and transform the lives of people all across, all wherewithal and other necessary means will be taken care of by the Universe endlessly. This is the basic premise of the law of Karma and its service to humanity. Your thought must precede your action and the subsequent reaction follows action. The whole process of thought-action, reaction, feelings, and emotions are the result of the ceaseless efforts of your creative mind as you continue to vibrate on the high frequency with a great amount of energy, frequency, and emotions. Throughout you have been passionately involved with plenty of emotions as you have formed a mental image of your desired 'goal', 'vision' and this new mental image has shifted your mental paradigm completely and the same has been programmed into your subconscious mind from there it can be communicated to the infinite source easily and effortlessly and through a self-transcendence. Here is a catch you have two power simultaneously working toward your goal one is you within you and the other is infinite intelligence. Your 'goal' and vision will be taken care of by the forces within and the infinite source. Your success will be a foregone conclusion.

# Chapter 12

# IMAGINATION

"Imagination is everything, it encircles the world."

Albert Einstein

The power of imagination is so vital that it continues to create and recreate mental images and mental pictures of desired goal and vision that you can feel the joy and live the moment of celebration as you envision your goal, vision being met.

The mind takes you where you want to stretch it, either in an ocean of despair and despondency or an ocean of happiness and ecstasy, but in both the spheres you need to control your propensities and impulsive thoughts to be at the helm of things. You can get away with the former by the way of imagination and resorting to the mental picture of your desired goal, as this will shift your focus and take away your energy toward your desired target. That is why the dreams, goals, and visions in life are so important, as they put you into an unknown voyage, but in a predictable situation. They give you the meaning of life and its existential value and without any goal, mission, or vision in life, one can easily get lost in the day today humdrum of life and is far away from the self and true potential. As Mark Twain writes "Sail away from the safe harbor, explore, dream, desire."

The real power lies in the present moment, not the past or future. The present moment is all that you ever have so make the most of it. Every second that passes us becomes the past in this timeless universe, as the difference between the present and past is of a nano second. We do not think about what we think?. To avoid misery and any chaos you have to start yourself from within, take charge of your inner self-deep down and as a whole, connect to your inner self with an ression of gratitude to the self and the who.  The fog, which is overshadowing your mind and your mechanical habits, is the conditioning that makes you the prisoner of the past. The mind is easily swayed by whatever crosses or blurs your vision, thoughts, and images you build. It remains constantly active and the waking mind itself remains in different states since it is entangled with your body and there is a rapid flow of energy and information and it reacts to the situation as it arises and builds up a defense mechanism.

The power of imagination is so vital as it gives you the meaning and essence of your being. The imagination comes from the consciousness and it is essential to broaden your consciousness by the constant process of exploration of the other side and navigate within and other realms and get into its source and other dimensions. Here the realm of sixth sense comes into operation. The sixth sense, being those creative and profound insights that mold and guide and goads deeper within, offers you extended perspectives of life. It opens the doors of wisdom in this vast ocean of life and connects your finite being with the infinite. Imagination is so vital and imperative for creation. How can this faculty be sharpened? By constant use and elevation of your mind and connect to the unknown forces of different dimensions in this cosmos. It will give you feelings of well-being and put you in the path of action as you move toward your desired vision and goal.

Life is a mystery and is moving from imperfection to perfection, and the Mind is consciousness, and consciousness is the sign of creation. "Go confidently in the directions of your dreams, live the life you have imagined," writes Henry David Thoreau.

When you begin to raise your level of consciousness and vibrate high, you will develop the capacity and ability to receive information other than five physical senses, and through the sixth sense (extra sensory perception), at the psychic level also mind receives information. You can also develop the ability to have clear clairvoyance, which is the ability to see beyond the physical plane and clairaudience, hear sound and signal beyond the physical plane. That being the essence of high consciousness and the process of constant evolution.

As Henry David Thoreau writes so beautifully "You must live in the present, launch yourself on your wave, find your eternity in each moment."

Have you wondered when you experience extreme and complete joy when your imagination knows no limits and there is a boundless source of energy and an exquisite feeling even all small things make you laugh and cry and you tend to enjoy everything to the hilt? You experienced the joy of joys and you believed that life was magical with no beginning and end and all seems to flow at its flow and spontaneity. It was a time of childhood. The most treasurable and immeasurable time. Your entire existence floats in the ecstasy of joy, happiness and you enjoyed every bit of creation. As you grow and take the existential journey, things begin to change, your being is bombarded and infused with all sorts of beliefs,  get conditioning in all spheres of life such as physical, mental, and spiritual, and accordingly, your sense of faculties and imagination start to develop. All your thoughts, emotions, feelings have the effect of your conditioning,  it sets the sense of direction and frames your mental paradigm based on your habits,  conditioning, and the internalization of the                     entire                     process.

# Chapter 13

# THE COSMOS AND THE CREATION

"In all Chaos, there is a Cosmos, in all disorder, there is a secret order."

Carl Jung

The Cosmos is an interplay of cosmic energy and we are put in this unknowable world. From time immemorial, man has been quite inquisitive and in the process of seeking beyond the physical and materialistic world, something, infinite, unlimited, and ultimate sacred. This yearning desire and longing push humans into the possibility of something beyond known into the unknown. The experience and the understanding of both the mundane and spiritual world and persistent spiritual voyage with the combined scientific and medical knowledge and research has not led to any concrete or convincing belief about the infinite source. The guesswork of the Neuroscientists more specifically of those who worked on the mind and brain power and brain's relations vis a vis the mind is quite mind-boggling. They did try to get into the uncharted territory of the mind without realizing that mind exploration is more of experience and realization and the mind is part of one's consciousness. Any thought or any idea that germinates in the mind navigates all the way across and gets electromagnetic waves from the brain before the same being is fructified into action. This all happens in the consciousness domain. The intellectual exploration might go down from macro to extreme micro-level of any cell structure possible to the formation of first life in the form of chemical dust followed by microbes to single cellular amoeba and so on this planet. This only seemed to suggest the possibilities and not exact realities of the time but the same could be known as one of the models of reality. These are the questions left unanswered by the science and the scientists, as there is no mechanism or method which they could authenticate about the mind, consciousness, thought, and how it operates and originates. The man who experiences and realizes it through the intense power of meditation and self-realization is the man who knows and can perceive anything between stones and the stars. The cosmos is inclusive of millions of galaxies, the Sun, the Stars, the Planets, the Sky, and the vastness of the creation is not an easy game for the human mind as this mystery can only be revealed by the cosmic mind. So, where the medical or scientific research ends, spiritual science begins to unravel the mystery of the unknown.

As D.H. Lawrance so beautifully says, "We and the cosmos are one, the cosmos is a vast body of which we are still parts. The sun is a great heart whose tremors run through our smallest veins. The moon is a great gleaming nerve center from which we quiver forever. Who knows the power that?"

Life means flow,  it is organic and dynamic and creativity is certainly one of the aspects of human life and one must strive for the development of intellect and wisdom which is the highest treasure of human beings and distinguishes humans from animals. As Socrates says "Creation is man's immortality and brings him nearest to the God".

To bring more creativity,  one must connect to the future from now moment and emotionalize the possibility of the desired goal, vision with enthusiasm and excitement and for more supreme and benevolent things, which expands human life generally as you crave for the manifestation of the highest human excellence and glory. In this moment of self-expression, deeper introspection as you develop a connection with your consciousness, this transmutation of your energy with the cosmic consciousness, you get spiritual experiences and sudden flashes and this constant pursuit of knowledge, awareness, where intuition begins and you enjoy your future moment in the present 'now'. Since your mind, consciousness has amalgamated with the supreme consciousness thereby leaving no scope to the creator and creation and liberated yourself. Yourself by your mind consciousness has crossed this existential rubicon and perceive it as the call of the great awaking and awareness.

The irony is that we think too much about the past and the future and do not think about the present moment at all. Live and be indulgent in the present moment as it is the only time you will ever have with all your aspirations and possibilities and confirm your inner voice and calling. You are consistent with yourself, your body, and your consciousness, which is in the process of transcending into other areas and you get answers within. How should one be in a creative state? The mind is the most delicate, ultimate thing of all creation which has been bestowed with all intellectual faculties with an inconceivable powerful thinking capacity as it keeps navigating in the cosmos and beyond time and space and is a part of the cosmic mind. It is here that those certain sudden creative insights appear since there is an amalgamation of waves of this mind with the cosmic mind. If these faculties are not used, they may become dormant and slide into the daily routine, the rut of life. You must know that your existence is meaningful only when you touch the highest point of creation and get into the stage of re-creation. To be creative, get the freewheeling of ideas, apart from being the highest vibrations, you must establish a connection with the infinite source, the creator, the cosmic mind wherein you can derive or extract energy from this infinite source and in the process, your search for meaning in life or existence might be answered. Creativity has no limits. In these moments of deep introspection and self-expression, you tend to go beyond deep within and try to seek the answer through your intuitive faculties like imagination, precognition. At their best, things will begin to flow at their level, events start unfolding. You know the purpose of your being. This may lead to self-transcendence at the psychical and more of self-aggrandizement at the physical level. The whole process of mindfulness and interplay of your thought waves will merge with the playfulness nature of the 'creator' and the creation, which are nothing but the subtle energy of the playful of the cosmic creation. The confluence and confusion of your thought energy waves with that of cosmic energy is a centripetal force and by cause and effect. The most eternal effulgence will shine and man will attain its full glory in pursuit of life based on more direct specifically directed actualized thought followed by persistent action and the mind has to be the complete controller of the entire gamut of activities and action. To control and master your mind, it is essential to get into the unknown kingdom of the Divine or infinite source, as this source will bestow its vast bound of energy, which will fructify into a huge and lasting source of abiding prosperity. Wholesome creative creativity and your spirit soar, your dreams become attainable, easily, and effortlessly achievable.

A paradigm shift happens due to a change in attitude and habits.  Mental waves keep changing depending on the frequency you are vibrating,  if you are thinking absolute negative crude form, accordingly your mental paradigm will be formed, which will then shape your behavior and the same will be solidified into a habit. A Paradigm is a mental program that has exclusive control over habitual behavior. The expression of the mind (hatred, fear, anxiety, etc). These expressions are negative and they have a vital role in the inner landscape and have an effect on your glands like the pineal and pituitary glands, which are very important to the body. The paradigm shift tames the mind in the right way and you can fully live in the present moment and enjoy the wholesome existential creation.

Albert Camus says **"I do not know whether this world has a meaning that transcends it. But I know that I do not know that meaning and it is impossible for me  just now  to know it"**

Chapter 14

# TIME, MIND, AND TIMELESSNESS

"Time is thin current slides away, but eternity remains."

Henry David Thoreau

Time is nothing but timelessness. There is no such thing as time, as it pervades in the consciousness. Time is an idea and if you do not think about it, it will die out in the mind. What is the time? Where does the time go? Is it eternal? As it is only captured in a frame and put in the cyclic motion just to run our lives, it can be viewed as Cyclical. "The Book of Genesis tells the story of the origin of the world and other narratives of the Bible – among them the Apocalypse or the Revelation of St. John- describes the end of the time. Time is the condition for the existence of the existence. Time is an essence for the realization of one's reality, which in itself is relative. What is true for you may not be true for others and vice versa. The Bible talks about the notion of linear time, with the beginning and an end, unlike the East, which believed in the idea of Cyclical time. Time is perennial and permeates through one's

69

consciousness and it is a state which dies at the moment of death at an individual level but without consciousness.

There is an entanglement of time, mind, consciousness, and timelessness, since all are relative, organic, stretchable, eternal, and timeless, no one could destroy them and all of them are masters of their play of any given time, space, and person, circumstances and events and runs the process of life to the whole and eventually becomes the part of the whole. The greatest certainty of the time is its uncertainty, and so is the uncertainty of the Universe and its other dimensions which are beyond the fabric of space and time. All this seems to be the cosmic play of the cosmic mind and is a big mystery to the human mind.

John Milton writes in paradise lost, "A man cannot be changed by place and time, the mind as its place, and in itself can make a heaven of hell, hell of heaven."

When you have dreams or goals to meet and reach with the consummating,  burning desire and the picture of your goal is painted in your mind, it would keep you in action mode. It is important to keep working and focus on the process and means as much as the result. You must flash your memory and mind with the picture of your dream and goal and feel, emotionalize the result, and feel the moment of its completion once or twice daily. Be enthusiastic, generate deep emotions and great feelings and stay calm happy and keep thinking and reminding even parroting about the desired goal or project undertaken. This constant repetition and thinking make the whole process easy, and further, it inspires you and the result seems more and more real.

You must be connected with your inner consciousness. You need to constantly navigate and cycle around in your entire mental dynamics and paradigm for the mission and the projects you had undertaken since you and your mind have formed a new self-image, new dynamics with new roles, and there is a great deal of self-acceptance, gratitude, appreciation love, and compassion not only for yourself but equally for other people humanity as a whole. You will realize that you are the creator's most marvel creations and you are part of the universal consciousness. The energy, and when your real being, self, and the from are nothing but merely a speck, a molecule of cosmic mind and creation and your being is part of the entire whole and in your moments of self-expression, awareness, and self-realization has got a clarion call of your soul, spirit to express yourself and goad into the endless possibilities of your being, which is dynamic, organic, and in the process creating something real tangible moving from state of duality to a-duality (non-duality). These startling changes and the metamorphosis of entire being is the only account of self-actualization and self-realization, which makes the entire existential journey and the process meaningful and life has a  meaning till the last moment in the scheme of 'God's creation, the soul and the consciousness, which is eternal and timeless in the evolution of cosmos thereby completing the cycle of creation,  and recreation combining all dimensions of micro and macro cosmos and going beyond the fabric of time and space into timelessness.

It is worthwhile to connect and vividly remember the great moments you have experienced in past, good times and simultaneously connect with the emotion of the future moments of creation that you envisioned and charted in your mental paradigm. The amalgam of both the emotion and a surge of waves in your consciousness will generate and recreate the emotional energy waves surging into your sub-consciousness mind. At this stage, you need to connect with your mind and with the infinite source through constant ideation and elevation of your inner self, soul. Seek the answer from within.  "Do not let the noise of other's opinions drown out your inner voice," says Steve                                               Jobs.

# Chapter 15

## LIVING IN THE PRESENT MOMENT

"Do not dwell in the past, do not dream of the future, concentrate the mind on the present moment."

Buddha

It is important to live in the 'now' moment. The time you ever have is just now and that too is fleeting by. One must get most of the present now moment to experience the full sense of being, at all levels physical, psychic and spiritual. How should one generate and create that state of connectedness with your being and in the process with the infinite source? Soak yourself fully in the present moment, deep down, and soar your mind through the process of stillness and utter silence in a meditative way, as you feel more and more emptiness and nothingness. Feel as you are an existential entity as part of this creation since your consciousness is vibrating on a higher level and there is a perfect rhythmic correlation between the mind, body, and the brain. As you are stretching yourself into the unknown from the known, you are feeling as if the whole creation is nothing but part of the consciousness. As you feel and occupy space at the spatial level and experience the passage of time and you feel that your existence is ephemeral but cannot delude yourself from the phenomenon of space and time. Your entire being is entirely the part of other larger dimensions of the infinite source and as you seem to experience this experience of this powerful subtle wave of energy of the infinite. This magnificent voyage throws your mental paradigm into the timelessness universe. At this stage, all your conceptual and perceptual, intuitive, imaginative activities are an inextricable part of the infinite as you are at the exalted stage of your being and about to touch the golden rubicon of the superconscious mind and attained the stage of self-realization and seem to know everything. That is how the Cosmos, self, time, and space are inscrutable entities and so are the human spirit, soul, and consciousness. Science seems to have no accurate answer for them and cannot measure them but the person having realized it through self-knowledge and self-realization can. The humans and the entire Cosmos are subservient to the witnessing entity, the infinite. Humans, science, and scientists are in the process and the least they could do to explore, the models of realism but won't have a clear-cut answer to these mysteries for all times to come. They must enjoy the mystery.

Each one of us has been bestowed with unseen and unique power and infinitely powerful subtle energy which required first to be realized and then channelized through a proper process of self-awareness and awakening. You need to submit yourself to the process of  Divine source sitting in a quiet, composed, serene place and imagine yourself be a loner on the planet for a while as you set your spiritual thermostat in order.  In this process there is renewal and retrieval of your vivid memories and as past mental pictures will flash across as you concentrate and move from temporal to extra-temporal and open your mind to the infinite source, the 'providence'.  As you deeply concentrate and raise your frequency, you route and navigate your energy through an inner landscape in high frequency and vibration as your consciousness is connected to the cosmos and the infinite source and you can seek answer and guidance of your herculean problems and set your inner dialogue in motion through prayer.  You have reached a stage that has opened the door of infinite possibilities and you continue to practice this and allow yourself to be connected like this daily for half an hour or so in complete calm and still moment.  This entire practice and repetition have also permeated into your subconscious mind, which will redirect, remake and redesign your entire being and make your journey sublime and easy.

Chapter 16

# THE MIND IS THE CONTROLLER OF EVERYTHING

"Rule your mind or it will rule you."

Horace, the Roman Poet

Your mind is the ultimate vehicle to take your desires and wishes and further to get them materialized. Your mind controls everything, from the micro to the macro levels of your thought creation. It is here that your thoughts start to germinate and are further processed as a dy

namite force by giving it definite shape and purpose through the principle of action, right attitude, and approach. The mind has always remained an unexplored territory. It is known for its prevarication, fast movement, flashes, murmuring, vividly past touching nostalgic moments, imagining future events, unfolding things due to change in mental paradigm. As you pass through events and exploration and travel through vicissitudes and the labyrinth of time, it might throw one to the other shores of time. The habitual conditioning of your complete being would have a cascading effect on your future course of action even what is seen and sensed, categorized, and memorized. You need to be in a stage of expectancy as you sense things through your perception and intuition. To overcome such fear and get out of an unwanted situation, the most important is to stop thinking negatively. Flood your mind with positive energy, imagery, other positive constituents to dilute your negatives feelings, emotions by changing your internal dialogue. You can attract things only when you feel utmost joy for the existence, equanimity, emotion of gratitude are high and when all your thought waves are aligned with the vastness of this creation. The negatives thoughts are more penetrating and magnetic and they seem to create more impact and effect on the human mind and get one down to an endless quagmire enough to create a chain of reaction in the entire inner landscape, dynamics and the result is complete chaos, dissension, and inner turmoil. The way to get out of it and surge ahead is by mastering your energy and working on your mental paradigm. The mental paradigm shift is imperative to get rid of negative thought patterns, situations. Once you learned the art of shifting your mental paradigm, there is going to be a huge drastic change in your entire being and everything seems to flow in the right direction. How apt are the sayings "Change your mind and change your life," "As a man thinketh, so he is" 'thoughts are things. To retract your mind from worldly pursuits, raise it to the highest level of vibration by way of silence and stillness. Practice it in a more happy and relaxed way and thoughtless condition. You must accept positive thoughts, feelings, emotions most of which are in tune with your desired goal, that makes you calm, happy, and are consistent with your wishes and desires. Talk to yourself, build your nest on lofty solitude. As rightly said by Schopenhauer "Loneliness is the fate of all outstanding minds." During this stage, you get connected to other dimensions and in these moments of calmness, you raise your vibrations and consciousness and seek the answers from the infinite source and express your wish or desire.  It is important to feel lighter, relieved,   and with equanimity, you feel empowered, expanded, and instantly supplement your mind with your desired goal and mental imagery and further cement the same with specific positive affirmation and imagine yourself to be right in that mental frame which you wished to be.  The entire process is full of intensity of extensity loaded with consumed feelings and your mind is constantly vibrating with high frequency and vibration and use your goal as a burning desire to reach the pinnacle of success. In this entire process, you must continue to seek refuge in the positive thoughts and the ocean of rhythmic waves, that are generated in the inner landscape of your dynamics.  This shift is almost akin to internalization, submerged and intoxicated with a high level of emotional energy. Which has been further permeated into the subconscious mind. Further when all seems hopeless, difficult, and desperate and have no strength of mind, then simply abandon all thought processes and get into thoughtlessness and trust the process of life and Divine intelligence with full surrender have an internal stillness and dialogue with the 'Providence'. As you do this with utmost faith, conviction, and surrender, all good and great are bound to happen. As the Bible says, "Faith and belief can move mountains."

There are umpteen instances wherein people have gone and experienced this situation due to bankruptcy in other areas of life, who have later been touched and catapulted with Divine Power, Divine spark and have their lives miraculously transformed. This is on account of dead faith in the creator, consistently and constantly taking time to connect with 'Him' whatever way one can and your silence will realize the essence of the totality of your being with the fond faith that the great architect and creator of the universe are in perfect harmony.

**As Spinoza says " Mind has an adequate knowledge of the eternal and infinite essence of God"**

# Chapter 17

# A PEACEFUL AND HARMONIOUS MIND

"Rhythm and Harmony find their way into the inward places of the soul."

Plato

A peaceful and harmonious mind is a productive mind. Human development must be harmonious at all levels. It is said that a healthy body has a healthy mind also. The mind to be more active, productive, and creative must be in a happy, calm, and tranquil state. Keep yourself busy and engaged with your pursuits besides all positive things and thoughts and laughter. As Albert Einstein writes "We must humbly admire the beautiful harmony of the structure of this world as far as we can recognize it at the moment and that is all."

There are ways and techniques, which are helpful, such as playing soothing music, painting pictures, any mural on the wall that inspires you, coupled with great quotes, taking walk near the beaches are also highly recommended as the surging and merging of sea waves are like the waves of your mind. They give meaning to the whole creation, just like how the waves of the ocean are hastening towards its shore and so are the waves of the mind, surging and merging with the cosmic waves of cosmic consciousness as both the sources are perennial, timeless, and endless. It is interesting to see that both life and water have a symbiotic relationship, as life without water is a complete impossibility.  Taking a solitary walk, far from the maddening rush, having a mountain view, staring at the sky from a solitary hilltop or full-moon night and stars view, engaging with a mastermind group of like-minded people,  engage in simple, easy positive conversation. Just take a walk down the huge thick forest, the rustling of leaves will have a soothing effect and the chirping of the birds will stir the music of the soul and the setting of the Sun will put you in silence, stillness, and gratefulness.    As John Milton has beautifully written in Comus, "One sip of this will  bathe the drooping  spirits in delight, beyond the bliss of dream."

The mind must be completely emptied of all cobwebs of daily existential worries, fears, anger, hate, resentment, anxiety, lust, etc; The best possible exercise we must practice or carry out to flush out all the negatives is to withdraw yourself completely from the mundane physical world and get into the state of the nothingness zero stage meaning thereby, to withdraw your mind from the physical world completely and feel that you are sitting as a single unit or entity in the Cosmos.  As you sit and meditate with this state of mind with emptiness, you will be able to concentrate bit by bit daily and after a month or so (maximum 3 months) a perceptible change in your overall being will begin to appear.  The mind will be conditioned altogether differently, supplement this with good books, kinds of literature you love to read and other ancient great books besides the Bible, the Koran, the Bhagavad Gita, the Guru Granth Sahib have strong therapeutic values.  Recall and remember the good inspiring times, beautiful experiences, and associations of your life.  The music played,  the song sung, the dance attempted, spiritual congregation attended or any passing past and present encounters, just learn to balance the internal dynamics and energy by meditation and self-consciousness.  You have to establish yourself in your higher consciousness and all the desires fulfillment come to you as all the rivers flow into the  Oceans ( as stated in the Bhagavad Gita in one of the verses.)  It is important to paint your mind with soothing thoughts and pictures, which calm your mind. We live in this dichotomous world, there is the duality of mind, the mind is divided and scattered in more than one direction. You need to get rid of this duality and dividedness and concentrate on single positive thoughts or divert all the propensities toward singleness one positive goal. Prayer or  Meditation is the best refuge to calm the mind and being in harmony with the vast source of creative energy. As Thomas Carlyle said, "Silence is the element in which great things fashion themselves". Prayer and prayer full mind, meditation is like a laser beam, strong subtle energy as it gets connected with the infinite intelligence, you have to drop and merge your thoughts and dissolve into higher consciousness. You need to be steadfast and have no mercy on yourself and consummate yourself with a single positive thought, get into the repetitive act of incantation, just as the rustling of the leaves as you walk down the well-grown planted area. This will take you in the ocean of positive waves of energy and you will be at peace in your heart and mind. As you connect with the higher source in a deeper sense of gratitude and this process you will have many realizations, self-awareness, and spiritual awakening.

Chapter 18

# THE MIND AND MINDFULNESS

"Mindfulness means being awake and knowing what you are doing"

The Mind is like an ocean of waves of energy, consciousness includes on its ambit many cognitive faculties, like, imagination, perception, intuition, thinking, intelligence, memory, judgment, willpower, reasons, emotions, instinct, etc; To take control of your thought process you need to work on a mental paradigm to control the negative thought pattern, if you are caught up in the whirlpool of negative thoughts, how to replace and shift the same, it is the thought which can bring dynamic, organic as well as any functional changes. As Maxwell Maltz writes so beautifully, "That mental attitudes can influence the body's healing mechanism, Placebos or Sugar pills & capsule containing invert ingredients have long been a medical mystery, they contain medicine of no kind that could bring about a cure". You have to be in the moment and feel and being aware of the moment or state of being consciously involved with the moment or act. Mindfulness must be practiced and pay full attention to your thoughts, emotions, and vibrations, which tames and involves the mind and brings it into the present moment.

The mind has gigantic, mysterious, miraculous potentialities and its capacity is unknown. It is estimated that the man 's using a small fraction of his mind, the maximum is ten percent and on average it could be less than four percent. This unexplored gold mine if tapped fully will change the self dynamics and the landscape of any nation in its entirety. The majority of it has no clue what they are doing where they are going and are mostly preoccupied with daily routine, and other anxieties, worries, negatives, guilt, and all sorts of other false notions, false sense of pride and prejudice that all has been going on since long and the mind got conditioned due to aforesaid reasons. To channelize such a vast source of energy and make use of your full genius, you need strong, confirmed, determined, cold blood acts daily. It is viable to have those actions in the early morning when you woke up preferably at 5 AM. This you could start with the belief that where are you right now and where would you like to go? That must be clear to you. Once that target is set in the form of a goal. You may be anything you would like to be making million dollars, getting your dream house in the space, any mission or dream for your country or humanity, anything you like to establish must clearly and specifically written on a piece of paper or card. That card must become your daily morning mantra to be embedded in your mind and is a kind of daily habit as you wake up and hit the ground first consciously for few weeks then it will take the form of routine. The whole process will also get planted in your subconscious mind as you do these routine mental activities daily. This would further strengthen your subconscious beliefs and same would act as a facilitator toward your desired goal. This is how you used your mind toward your intended goal. It is with persistent efforts and focus without any distraction. In this process you have done nothing, simply pushed and activated your mind for your desired goal, vision, or mission in life, which is real food for the mind. Since you have not used your mind and its faculties for any other creative work than the regular humdrum activities of the day, the genesis of the mind is in complete dormancy. It is as simple as just you need to examine something within your body to be in good health and stay healthy so as the mind needs to be activated and put to action for the realization of your worthy ideals and vision in life.

The mind can be tamed and trained to perform the tough task or use it properly for goal-related activities with the methodology given hereinabove. In this process, you will be able to make use of mental processes, faculties and that are vibrating on a higher frequency, and these vibrations stretching you from the known to unknown. The societal norms, beliefs, conditioning, newspaper reports, gossiping neighbors, friends one and all daily interaction, environmental and genetical conditions, on which your thought process has been conditioned, would sabotage every attempt of your new set mental paradigm unless you do not wish to act upon in a cold blood way and determine to do so for your dreams, visions or goal. All you need is to dream high, soar high, vibrate high and held the ground tightly, and live lightly. If you are steadfast and madly consummated with your goal with strong conviction and belief,  no power on earth can come in the way of your goal. The power of the mind is like a loadstar, it will take you where you wish to go, the sky and the beyond. When you are so immersed in the present moment, you are in the state of flow, peak performance, and maximum                                        productivity.

# Chapter 19

## SILENCE AND THE ESSENCE OF SILENCE

"Silence is the language of God."

Rumi

Free your mind from thoughts, empty it, and get into silence to get answers to few questions. Once you are in proper silence, try to connect to your inner being with the infinite. Merge your consciousness with the witnessing entity. This state of silence with equanimity, tranquillity, and serenity being in harmony with your being and is fully in sync with your existence. As you sit in this form of formless, feel your body is in perfect alignment with the Universal energy and consciousness. You can cherish the treasure of good memories of the past really good ones, which gives you a feeling of wholeness. It empowers you and moved from this place to the other dimension as you connect yourself with the higher source of infinite power and you have taken refuge in the eternal abode. This transcendental immortal consciousness is the expression of the divinity and ocean of timelessness. Your mind transcends all mental limitations. 'There is no permanency in the impermanent'. Your all dormant faculties become active in this great moment of silence, peace, and calmness. The essence of material pleasures and pursuits, bricks and mortars of this material world holds not much meaning and one gets beyond and your soul has reached a higher state of consciousness. In other words, "self-actualization is possible only as a side effect of self-transcendence" writes Viktor E. Frankel in his book 'man's search for meaning'. Mind moves from crude to subtle and in the process of self-actualization and self-transcendence, you are destined to merge your consciousness with cosmic cognitive faculty with a dual mission of self-transcendence and the universal love personified and the intended purpose with great responsibility, a desire and aim to accomplish a particular mission in life and tend to take life's inevitable, ups and down with grace, acceptance, and equanimity.

As you realize the expansive, essential knowledge of your spirit and your being, you get into a state of easiness and at the quiescent and in complete harmony with the whole, getting into the totality of creation, you become part of the larger consciousness in this whole play of things. In this cycle of labor and leisure–time, you get into the state of timelessness. By being part of the whole and man being only universal consciousness, the speck of dust at the time of conception until the process which did not happen and this would take time to evolve him or her complete real human being. As Thomas Carlyle said, "In silence, things emerge at length, full-formed and majestic, into the delight of life, which they are henceforth to rule". It is stillness, which stretches and broadens your inner being and you do not feel lonely and the entire universe is inside you. As Rumi says "Still, be still and listen".

The entire process begins with dynamic and creative force while you are on a continuous journey the lone word faith and beliefs to yourself. Hold these words into your conscious mind and let them permeate into your subconscious mind. The mind is to be impregnated with high positive energy from different sources and scriptures, selfless services, and gratitude. It is important to connect with your inner self. The entire process will recondition your mind and it would become fertile and nurture new thoughts. As you know where you would like to be in this vast body of creation. You just need to harbor this wish, desire of reaching there. The clarity of goal and direction will pave the way and you would enjoy the journey at its best. It is as strong and cataclysmic as like the sea waves surging ahead with all its might kissing the pebbles on the shore same is the case with your journey on the way as your will, desire, faith, belief and the force of incantation and the divine connection will propel and you would be driven toward your goal, as there is no chance of drift and shift all along as your energy is fully concentrated and is like a laser beam.

It is essential to keep your mind quiet and empty also of unwanted thoughts of anger, hatred, irritation, frustration, stagnation, and annoyance. These negative, unhappy, and unpleasant thoughts need to be flushed out periodically by the constant practice of mediation, silence, and consistent bombardment of positive energy by reading good books, audio talks, divine prayer. The mind needs to be equally drained out like that of the body which equally needs the removal of toxins and organs rejuvenation fortnightly by way of fasting giving rest to the body organs. The mind-body rejuvenation and relaxation are vital for the process of re-creation and vice-versa. In this process of re-creation and relaxation, there is self-awareness and awaking and a constant flow of energy from within to a larger whole, the mind, body, cosmos involved. This entanglement of energy as a result of the grace of the Divine is supremely needed to banish the other profanities and give and grant you the blessing which you conceive and believe. The dynamics of the universe works on its Divine plane and the enormous energy the Universe possesses, so is the case with the human mind, a gigantic force of energy. This cohesion of energies of Divine and human are complementary to run the cycle of creation and re-creation. This unique gift of the mind and its faculties of intuition, insights and vivid sense of memory, and fantastic sense of imagination bestowed on humans to goad deeper within and touch the other dimensions of cosmos and its creation. In any event, if there is a profusion of your mind and cosmic mind, you are sure to hit the cosmic button of liberation or salvation. Even if you fail short of it, your genius is bound to flash out like the Buddha, or anyone who could tame the world with your all-pervasive knowledge.

<u>Chapter 20</u>

## LAW OF OBSESSION

"To succeed, work hard, never give up and above all cherish a magnificent obsession."

Walt Disney

Human life is precious and so is its presence in the given limited period on this planet. What noble thing you could accomplish so that other start deriving benefit from that.? This you need to be clear since time is an essence you cannot stretch your life, you own and consume this passing moment. You must be clear on your purpose and other dimensions of life. You must elevate yourself to a level where you feel grateful and in abundance, in the process elevate others to reach their high potential. If you make an impact and any contribution to societal well-being, you lived the life of purpose, your life reaches its highest form and glory.

W. Clement Stone writes "I have a magnificent obsession. All I want to do is to change the world, make it a better place for this and future generation" The law of obsession simply amalgamates you with your vision and goal through your passion and consuming, burning desire. It straightens your attitude to accomplish something bigger in life. It charters new territory and the distance you wish to cover and navigate across to reach the established desideratum. You need to be attracted and obsessed with your vision and goal.  All you need to be disruptive to the old hardened patterns of your thoughts and deconstruct the hardened beliefs and attitudes to create a new mental paradigm. This shift would entail the formation of new thoughts, habits, and actions.  This would create a new perspective and cultivate new habits that will make your life far richer and more meaningful and would not let you deviate or distract under any circumstances as the entire process has been internalized.   As the celebrated author, Napoleon Hill writes "Your ability to use the principle of autosuggestion will depend  very largely upon  your capacity to concentrate upon a given desire until that desire becomes a burning obsession"

## ATTITUDE AND GRATITUDE

"Our attitude toward life determines life's attitude towards us."

John N. Michell

"If I have seen further than others, it is by standing upon the shoulders of giants."

Isaac Newton

The above two most powerful words have a great impact on the lives of people.  The attitude of a person determines his victory or failure. This is so profound that to have success in life, the right attitude is important. It is so fair and clear that if you change your mental attitude, you can change your life and so are the situation, circumstances, and places that would favor you accordingly. William James, the father of American Psychology, who was also a professor of Psychology at Harvard, writes "The greatest discovery of my generation is that human beings can alter their lives by altering their attitudes of mind". As you think so you shall be, it is vital that your thinking pattern changes, when situations, circumstances, and places demand. You cannot run the system, things, even Nation with worn-out ideas and ideology. It has to change per the dynamics of time, nation, and societal needs. Sometimes it so happens in life or the workplaces it is only your attitude that shapes your success and failures. The statement by the prolific author William James is so apt today and even at all times to come. As you move high on the professional ladder, the success would largely depend on your attitude in all stages such as personal, impersonal, and organizational levels. There is no easy cakewalk, no inflexible and inbuilt mechanism would work or help if you do not possess the right attitude. It is a sine qua non and vital for sailing through the troubled times and it is inextricably linked with your desired vision and goal. The right attitude will keep you ahead and on a high pedestal put you on a high trajectory in all dimensions of life concerning physical, mental, psychic, and spiritual. It is with this mental frame or paradigm, you will make a difference and would be far ahead of others. The two magic words attitude and gratitude are the connecting links of where you are now at this moment and to the life of your dreams or the future, you envisioned. The attitude of mind is like your behavior and the response and your reaction to the external stimuli or situation. **As Victor E. Frankl elegantly writes "Between**

**stimulus and response there is a space. In that space is our power to choose our response. In our response lies our growth and our freedom"** How deep your attitude determines your success and failures in all your pursuits of life. Your attitude so to say must be relative must correspond to the situation and external stimuli, soft, simple, brute, crude, ruthless, aggressive, regressive, calm, cool, easy, and relaxed. It is depending upon the kind of situation you are in. Your attitude has to do with the situation of life, events, and circumstances. Gratitude is a feeling, is a kind of energy, the deeper you have, the more expansive you will become in terms of health, wealth, relations, and other necessary things in the life of which you are indebted. The grateful heart and right attitude are open and receptive to change and fit into any situation, circumstance, and event. The magic mantra is to have an extremely positive attitude with cold blood acts along with deliberate and spontaneous feelings of gratitude for life, creation, and the Universe. The more abundance you receive, it opens the more possibility of more abundance. The right attitude with utmost gratitude, an act of kindness and generosity and service to humanity for all you have, and to the cosmos and its creation including all animate and inanimate objects is the strength of your soul and consciousness is one of the highest purposes and highest dimensions of your life. As John Milton writes about gratitude "gratitude bestows

reverence, allowing us to encounter everyday
epiphanies, those transcendent  moments of awe
that change forever how we experience life and
the                                        world."

# Chapter 22

## CONCENTRATION OF THE MIND

"Concentration of consciousness are of its essence."

William James

Any electrifying idea or thought as soon it is germinated in the mind instantly jotted down on paper. The moment it is written the messages goes to the brain through a nerve.  It would remain as dominant, primary thought will not be overwritten by the subsequent thought, since the mind would be constantly bombarded by series of thoughts. The same thought then permeates into the subconscious level and is embedded there, the same thought has traveled into three layers first from the conscious level to the brain, and then into the subconscious mind. While writing the mind, the brain, muscles, nerves images, visuals are in play. This gives an absolute sense of direction, intensifying the power of concentration and keep you focused on your goal, mission, and vision. Through the power of concentration, one becomes a more seeker of knowledge benefits and gains all possible knowledge. The Universe is ready to give all its secrets corresponding to your efforts and actions, but are you ready to receive it? Concentration is important to focus your mind on a point, it just aims to strive and arrive at a point to the exclusion of everything else. The mind is constantly on a run cannot hold it on a single subject unless concentrated. This is so in all areas of life, personal, professional, or spiritual. So, learn to concentrate your mind to gain control of the situation or life. This is a unique power human beings are endowed with besides other faculties and this is the main difference between men and animals. The higher the power of concentration the higher the levels of energy. The trained man and tamed mind never make mistakes. You have to polish and nourish your mind in such a way that is tuned to good vibrations and receptive to good thoughts. The entire Universe is in your mind and it is your mental attitude, which makes the world for you the way you entertain your thoughts. You must learn this art of controlling your mind and propelling it in the right direction, there is nothing that cannot be achieved.

As Napoleon Hill writes "Thoughts are things and powerful things when they are mixed with definiteness of purpose, persistence and burning desire and get translated into action". Thomas Edison was a great example who because of his great concentration of mind and a consuming burning desire and scores of others have achieved huge success. Despite his ten thousand failures, he went on and on and every failure describes near to success. This kind of mind comes with a mission and ambition to do something stupendous and something to give to society and work with single pursuit, devote their life, mind, heart, and soul to it. They are the true warriors and makers of their destinies. They get all money, wealth, richness, and happiness as they are focused, determined, and on a mission to do larger for societal interest.  As  Henry Ford says "you are master of your fate and captain of your soul". The road to the good and great is roughest and tough and your work has to pass through these stages of ridicule and opposition but their consuming obsession with their goal leaves no scope for failure.

What is that which vibrates from our levels of energy and sees images of future events sometimes? Strange are the ways of infinite intelligence and strange are the ways of our consciousness which penetrates and envision the kind of future for yourself and there is the energy behind every, thought, action, and the energy when released into the Universe and the thoughts mixed with emotions are magnetized and gets attracted and harmonized with a similar thought in the Universe.  The vibrant energy is harnessed through great conviction and faith. The same can be transplanted into the minds of common mass through the principle of strong autosuggestion and they have personified their energy into whole and may easily gain faith from millions of people all across. It is their idea which they could imagine and same to be easily identifiable with the people. They have become a beacon of light for humanity. The classic examples are  Martin Luther King, Jr. Nelson Mandela, Netaji Subhas Chandra Bose, Swami Vivekananda, and Mahatma Gandhi. They could see and imagine the outcome of their ideas.

# CHAPTER 23

## BIOCENTRISM & PERCEPTION

"If the doors of the perception were cleansed, everything would appear to mean as it is infinite."

William Blake

Your Consciousness creates the Universe. Could the Universe exist without Life? That means all are within consciousness. The consciousness is the main theme of a canvass that the whole is being projected and erected and without your consciousness, nothing exists. An American Medical Doctor and Scientist, Robert Lanza writes "nothing is perceived except the perceptions themselves, nothing exists outside of consciousness. Only one visual reality is extant, and there it is. Right there. The 'outside world' is, therefore, located within the brain or mind". The world seems to be an extension of your consciousness so is the time and space construct. In that event, it is a perceptional reality. The time, space constructs are on a physical domain to run the existential worldly affairs. The Big Bang and other theories suggesting the origin of the

Universe seem to give no clue and are guesswork, which does not stand the test of time. It seems that the cosmos has its origin based on its cosmological ectoplasmic profusion where the cosmic mind would have played its role. Since this is beyond the understanding of the ordinary human mind. If consciousness is the supreme and seems to be all-pervasive and powerful. If one could expand this consciousness through the process of awakening within and even then the grace of the cosmic mind is also needed to see that spark of enlightenment. This requires the liberation of your mind and attainment of self-knowledge knowing that only an eternal entity, to be the only goal of life, one has to propel one's mental propensities toward Him and in the process not mistaking the temporal for the eternal. This would come through the only process of self-knowledge and self-realization. Since our minds are finite could extend their frontiers to the possible limit unless the same is not intoxicated with the thought of the infinite, in that event the finite mind transcends its limits and goes into a state of endless and timelessness. That would answer the fundamental question of consciousness and its wholesome, countless vibrational undulations of the source energy. The solution of all lies deeper within. The individual consciousness will merge with the supreme consciousness to remove the dualism. The human mind is the cause of bondage and also same can be a cause of liberation. If the mind is crude, the entire existence of humans turns into crude matter.  If the movement of the mind is subtle, then it will move towards the infinite source.  The feeling of 'I' surrendered at the altar of source power or supreme existence, the entire existence will become one with source or supreme. One will become an omniscient and all-pervasive force. This takes the human consciousness with the supreme thereby smashing the concept of space and time.

Demonstrate faith and keep your consciousness raised, must be thoroughly soaked in the supreme ideation, do whatever capacity you can for larger interest, be humble, receptive, and learning all the time with no vanity. Feel the abundance, joyous, and gratitude that life has offered you a chance to be on this planet as a human being.

The Supreme consciousness is everywhere but vibration originates from God's nucleus and God's grace. You must be willing to lose everything to gain something far greater and bigger. You must know the purpose of life and the journey you have undertaken until this stage. In moments of your deeper and stillness process no matter what the situation and circumstances are, you need to be relaxed without doubt and fear, to be intelligent enough to tap and gauge the universal energy but not intellectual as it blocks success and question the infinite intelligence,  raises doubt and fear in your mind about the source and infinite mind, since your mind is not pure as it lashed with too much of intellectual toxicity and is not pure and is not traveling within but out. To get closer to the supreme consciousness and feel the presence of His psychic waves, the self of the individual within the layers of mind or existence has to be awakened through self-actualization and self-realization as the human existence is constantly evolving in the evolution of the Cosmos. If the universe is a perceptional reality for humans same might be the projection or imagination of the infinite or cosmic mind, can it be accepted as real? It is a relative truth.

What you ask for and seek, is given and found. If you hold petty, mean, selfish, shallow, envious, hateful, and greedy thoughts and the mind is conditioned and train in such a way and with such thoughts in minds, you can not experience and draw any power rather there is the denial of the universe and the Supreme. When you see and experience the vastness of the beauty of the cosmos and its creation and stretching your mind to that extent transcending into the other dimension with expanding awareness. The majority of us lead thoughtless life and easily allow our minds to decay. We realize this folly toward the middle or end of life when misery and sorrows seem to thickens and joy and pleasure shrinks. Positive and good thinking is essential for good living. As Stephen Hawking writes, "You cannot understand the glories of the Universe without believing there is some supreme power behind it."

In this entire journey, you are not alone,  your consciousness is part of the whole cosmic consciousness, it is more so when your consciousness is in the process of expansion and recreation,  wherein you enjoyed the process, willing to give yourself to others and others societal and humanity interests.  The universal creative energy transmutes its energy to the unit consciousness and presents its limitless possibilities which the subjective mind presents to us.  The Universal conscience has no mind of its own, it operates through your conscience and works on the law of expansion. Since the Universe is nothing but a bundle of energy of animate and inanimate objects and in this constant process of evolution man is on the highest pedestal and has been given inconceivable power of cognition, reasoning, perception, and imagination to fit into God's scheme of things. The cosmic cognition, intelligence works on its perfect plan and there is no disorder in its kingdom, the disorder created by the human intelligence and its creative faculties as it is working to create a model quite opposite to its form and being based on two realms of eternal and truth of absolutes and other relative factors, which seems paradoxical, as man has not attained that exalted sense of divine glorification nor mastered the principles of sixth sense and the mysterious higher power and also on the principle that 'Nature obeys us precisely in proportion    as    we    obey    first    Nature'.

Chapter 24

# DO NOT LET THE MUSIC DIE INSIDE YOU

"Do not feel lonely, the entire Universe is inside you."

Rumi

The one life and one time you are on this plant and must make most of it. Live life to the fullest whatever you wish to do must do and do not let fear stand in your way.  Since each day you live between the possible and an inevitable and you do not know when the 'Providence' would hit.

As Wayne Dyer put it so beautifully, "Do not die with your music still in you" So free yourself from all chains, express yourself fully, and celebrate life each moment. The journey of life is not always smooth sometimes one has to walk on rough edges, pass through many ups and downs. What exactly is life is?. You need to connect to the higher power to navigate through all vicissitudes of life.   Thank the

God, the Universe, the Sun, and the Creations.

 My thoughts seem to come from a great distance from the interior of my heart. The whole cosmos seems full of excessively melodramatic, megalomaniac, and idiosyncratic mortals. The false sense of vanity with ego is virtually decimating the entire existential humanism. To do away with this notion be indulgent, passionate, compassionate, and accept the supreme forces of the cosmic mind 's cosmic play in different dimensions and cosmology and evolution of the Cosmos and your inner calling. Find your purpose, passion, love and highest intrinsic values and priorities in life. Your inner dialogue and connection will give you a direction and there would be totality of the possibilities  in this universe. As Jean Paul-Sartre writes "Existentialism is a humanism" The life we have got is quite precious and given this golden chance to be born as humans,  why waste it in false absurd follies and all sort of profanities. Humanity is torn between ism and realism. The Universe is nothing but a cosmological drama, we the mortals are only actors doing our confined, assigned, and destined roles and then no more on the scene. Therefore, all forms of hypocrisy and other obnoxious acts targeted to demean and destroy human society are the results of our gross crudification of our thought process and the archaic thought and ideology we adhere to. These actions would have bearing on our existence as these are the seeds of our malicious and crude thoughts. Today is nothing but a projection of yesterday and yesterday is nothing but the creation of today and hence we are in this vicious circle. The difficult and terrifying question is 'self-knowing', the answer could be euphoric but slightly despondent, if you are 'indulgent' then you are you and if you are inert then you are naught. Create working space inside you with a bio-psychological, existential touch. The music inside you will compel everybody to dance to your tune, once you get it that is life and realism.

As the great Emerson writes  "Write in on your heart that every day is the best day of the year. No Man has earned anything rightly until he knows that every day is doomsday. Today is a king in disguise. Today always looks mean to the thoughtless, in the face of a uniform experience that all good and great and happy actions are made up precisely of these blank today. Let us not be deceived. Let us unmask the king as he passes."

"We look backward too much and look forward too much and thus miss the passing moment". William Lyons Phelps in 'one day at a time'

We are lost in the web of thoughts and do not use our innate capacity to the maximum.  As Albert Camus writes " Some of us may choose to be heroic, even knowing that will bring us neither reward nor salvation". Creative thinking refreshes the mind, rejuvenates and regenerates the new ideas gives you a winning feeling,  creative people probes, penetrates pushes the boundaries of close doors, intensely observant of the situation, probing and polite to the people around. The creativity is harnessed and sudden flashes of it reoccur.


 As Philosopher poet,  George Santayana writes, "There is no cure for birth and death save to enjoy the interval."

<u>Chapter 25</u>

# THE MIND AND TIME

"The Mind  once stretched by a new idea never returns to its original dimension."


R.W. Emerson


Did time exist without the mind?  Is it the perception of the human mind? Time may or may not be there before the existence of the Universe. If the Universe was not there how would Time be there? It seems time and Universe has a symbiotic relationship. As soon as the  Universe came into existence, so did time. It is the natural consequence of the creation of the universe or vice versa.  Since nothing has been proved and it is simply the guesswork of, physicists and scientists. Big bang seems to be an abstract proposition. It could not be proved and remained one of the mysteries of the time in this timeless universe.

We cannot change the moment of time and tide and but we can master the moment of our mind.

That is the reason time and mind are connected and time is a projection or extension of mind and mind that can cross the fabric of space and time. One must not get completely lost in the maze of life and cease being the slave of time. You will not be a slave of time once you have mastered your mind and its faculties. The frontiers of the cosmos in its timeless glory and waves of mind in its thoughtless motion and vibration are part of the cosmic consciousness are the creator's subtlest creations as both of them are not absolute themselves.

The Universe seems to be the projection of the cosmic consciousness and  'all the existential phenomena are emanated from the Cosmic Nucleus' of the divine infinite Source. The universe having been emanated as a self-contained phenomenon.

So on an individual level time seems to be an extension of your consciousness. Time operates through the mind more so when we are obsessed with the future and links it to the past also ignoring the present moment.  It is through spiritual inclination or constant practice our mind will develop in all states. Further, the power of conception and conceiving will also develop along with the faculty of intuition and cognition. These powers and faculty if harnessed properly would reveal us many secrets about coming events and circumstances,    and other cataclysmic global human crises threatening the human race and collapsing of the economic system. Sometimes it so happens that the subtle nature of certain deadly molecules might function within the world of perception through inferences such as touch, taste, form, smell, etc, and another category within the subtler world of the human mind. The human mind can overcome it and banish these phenomena using its power of consciousness.

When you are with yourself and inside deep down feels the vastness of creation and flow with the fullness of life, your inner wisdom guides you easily and effortlessly. There is the complete joy of the present moment and you are in complete harmony with yourself and the Universe. Your consciousness stretches on and on and deeper down gives you the meaning of the whole and there is oneness. Your wisdom is responding to you exactly what you wanted in life. No outer chaos disturbs your mental equanimity and equilibrium and you see a life full of possibilities as new seeds are germinated in the mind in harmony with the body mind and soul.

The inner space is like an ocean, flowing with different streams of thoughts, which are like oases in the desert of lost hope.

# Chapter 26

# THE MIND AND BODY BALANCE

"The body must be in an intimate relationship with the mind."

Albert Szent Gyorgi , Scientist

More than ever before, it is generally believed and scientifically proved that most of the diseases are 'Psychosomatic' and the illness is linked to the mind. The most mysterious gland in the human body is the Pineal Gland, located directly in the center of the brain. How to attain self-mastery through positive thinking? It is through prayer and meditation. Meditation is known to have caused an effect a great deal. It enhances concentration, ignores distractions, and gives you a feeling of peace and equanimity. It controls the wanderings of the mind and creates the mind body's perfect balance and increased the power of the mind and sharpens other faculties. It is essential to keep the  mind and body in perfect harmony and harmony with the cosmos and keep the mind calm and poised in all situations with high vibration as the calm mind is the savior of all the situations in the world and achievers of all visions and ideals as James Allen writes "your vision is the promise what you shall one day be; your ideal is the prophecy of what you shall, at last, unveil." Your body is a vehicle through which your mind operates and oscillates and with all your wisdom and all power, the mind is energized to perform the tireless and timeless activity in the Universe.

When your mind is calm, cool, and in high vibrations, it is the seedling of all your ideas and visions, creating new paradigms and realities aiming to navigate the unchartered territories. This stage of mind opens new vistas. As Rumi says "Just as the water reflects the stars and the moon, the body reflects the mind and the soul". When you are out of the daily rut and seemed to have embraced new things in form of habits, thoughts and there is a great deal of change in your mental paradigm and you have tamed, developed, and trained all your mental faculties such as reason, willpower, concentration, faith, intuition and imagination to help yourself in all corporeal and mental suffering. You must rely on intuition and gut instincts to further your decision and change the existing paradigm not conducive to yourself and the human race. You are operating on different levels of consciousness here and all the energy is being derived from the cosmic intelligence as all your mental faculties are aligned and in harmony with the universe and infinite source. You are in a position to realize your absolute being, which is an integral part of the infinite source, and in the process, you would be able to experience or realize the supreme entity. As poet Walt Whitman  so elegantly writes " There is that in me  I do not know what  it  is - but I know it is in me."

 Your inner self is awakening and there is a great deal of awareness and it enables the mind to rise above the physical and psychic level and guide into the world of cognition. Since you can conquer your mind through this process or process of meditation and you are a spiritual aspirant and believes in the supreme power. If you can capture and realize this supreme power and you are blessed with   His grace. You have attained your desideratum in all its form and manifestation.

The mind has never been trained and tamed and allowed to be conditioned most crudely and most of us regard earthly life as temporal vanity and don't dare to dream and nor cherish any vision not harbor any spiritual impulse in its fullness and allow the mind to navigate at a petty level.

It only takes little to dream, cherish, treasure, and open your consciousness as you hold everything in your consciousness, concentrate, ideate on your dreams, visions, and divine. In this frame of mind, you bloomed and blossomed and feel the eternal verities of life, and as you feel and live the life as if you have lived the life twice having no regrets whatsoever. This kind of consciousness would lead individuals and humanity to a greater level of wisdom and intellectuality. That is the power of the mind, time, and consciousness all three subtle sources of energy coming from the same source of supreme consciousness, which is eternal and timeless merging into the whole and cosmic consciousness. This is the supreme truth. The mind, the time, and the consciousness cannot be subjected to any frame, if they are to like mind and time into body and clock, these are the mediums through which the individual and the universe have to operate and run. These are the supreme parables are mysterious ways of the Divine, the Divine can only know to play and control the cosmos by its power of supreme cognition. I must conclude with the apt word of Socrates which states "As for me all I know is that I know nothing."

# Chapter 27

## MAKE YOUR MIND HAPPY

"I have learned never to underestimate the capacity of the human mind and body to regenerate even when prospect seems most wretched."

Norman Cousin

Always remember to look inwards and reorient yourself in moments of disbelief, depression, anxiety, fear, chaos, and confusion. Do not stretch your body and mind at that stage just be in the present moment. As R.L Stevenson says "Make up your mind to be happy. Learn to find pleasures in simple things"  Be away from addictions, distractions, let go of things that do not matter. Choose and make choices where to go and when to flow and set sail on life's vast ocean. You must know what you know, find a way and it will lead you to the highway. As beautifully written by  P.B Shelly "fear not for the future, weep not for the past" move on.  Be humble and honest and get connected with yourself. You never have the time, tide, moments, place, and loved ones waiting for you altogether. 'Is it a world, life, or time on whose last step you climb?. Sometimes' time is the storm in which we are all lost'  but always remember that the Sunsets to rise again.

  Losing and gaining is the game life always plays and it goes on, the mind would conquer what all you deeply, innately wished for and desired. By using the body and mind together in a harmonious way without any fear of death, the power of the mind can even defy and delay the predictable medical death by years and even other events, if you intensely wish so.

It was sometime in the year 2014-15  when my late wife, was diagnosed with carcinoma with an advanced prognosis of the last stage. However, she went on to live five years contrary to high expert Doctors' opinions of only surviving for six months.  She overcame all this through the sheer power of her mind and happiness. Soon enough, the full-body scan showed her almost disease-free, which baffled the medical experts in the field. This just goes to show us that the power of the mind can be used through your subconscious mind to vanquish and overcome anything. As Norman Cousin writes "The real tragedy of life is not death, but what we let die inside of us while we live".  It all starts in your mind,  the mind is to all human intellectual cognitive faculties and ability to comprehend and understand. Consciousness is the mental state of being awake. You need to bring change at the fundamental level of your existence and not at the superficial level. You must strengthen your subconscious beliefs in respect of whatever you desire or cure any disease coupled with other necessary things as no anxiety or fear of death should be there. You can delay or defy the events, people, and circumstances by using your power of mind and state of happiness. As Norman Cousin writes in 'Anatomy of an illness' "how humor and laughter and power of the mind can be used to heal your body". He was discovered with crippling life-threatening irreversible disease and went on to live full-fledged life contrary to the Doctor's opinion of six months or so.

That goes to show that human existence and consciousness are intimately attached. When you strongly desired to live with enthusiasm and celebration and laughter as these are subtle energy centers or molecules or contents of your consciousness and your mind moves towards the unknown, beyond space and time, the change begins to happen at every level of existence. As Leo Tolstoy writes "Seize the moments of happiness, love and be loved. That is the only reality in the world, all else is folly". You have to define the moment and yourself, not find yourself but create yourself. As Walt Whitman so beautifully writes, "Either define the moment or moment will define you."

These energy centers create a need for more life and you receive more life. ***Aseem Kr. Katoch***